GREAT
SPIES
of the
WORLD

JOHN PERRITANO

red rhino
b**OO**k s®
NONFICTION

Area 51

Cannibal Animals

Cloning

Drones

Fault Lines

Great Spies of the World

Hacked

Monsters of the Deep

Monsters on Land

Seven Wonders of the
Ancient World

Tuskegee Airmen

Virtual Reality

Witchcraft

Wormholes

SADDLEBACK
EDUCATIONAL PUBLISHING
www.sdlback.com

ISBN-13: 978-1-68021-049-1
ISBN-10: 1-68021-049-1
eBook: 978-1-63078-368-6

Printed in Malaysia

20 19 18 17 16   2 3 4 5 6

TABLE OF CONTENTS

Chapter 1

IN THE DEAD OF NIGHT

It is 1:00 a.m.

The army base is quiet.

A woman creeps onto the base.

She makes no sound.

She has a job to do.

Secrets to steal.

She walks into the general's office.

She is scared.

Spying is risky work.

The woman turns on the computer.

She types in the password.

Files appear.

She only wants one.

It has plans.

Plans to a top-secret weapon.

She puts in a memory stick.

Begins to copy the file.

She's not a *traitor*.

That's what she tells herself.

But she needs money.

So she has to steal secrets.

Footsteps.

She looks up.

A guard is checking the doors.

Her heart races.

The file finishes downloading.

The plans are hers.

She ducks under the desk.

Time ticks by.

The guard passes.

That was close.

Too close.

The woman sneaks away.

The base is soon behind her.

She heads to a park.

A man stands there.

She walks up to him.

He asks for the plans.

She laughs.

She wants the money first.

Then things go wrong.

Sirens blare.

Lights flash.

The man runs away.

The woman is alone.

Cars pull up.

A voice yells, "Hands on your head!"

Her spying days are over.

Spies are real.

They steal secrets.

Lie about who they are.

It is not a safe job.

They can go to jail.

They can die.

To some, spies are *criminals*.

To others, they are heroes.

It all depends which side you are on.

Chapter 2
I SPY

Spies steal secrets.

From whom?

Governments.

The military.

Businesses.

SPY LINGO: MOLES

Some spies are called moles. Moles are animals. They hide and dig in the ground. Spies dig for secrets. They hide too.

Spying is called *espionage*.

It is about getting *information*.

Things few know about.

Maps.

Battle plans.

Secret weapons.

Letters.

Some spies work for their country.

They want to help.

Protect it from enemies.

So they spy on other nations.

Get secrets.

Uncover plans.

Then they send the secrets home.

Others spy against their own country.

They don't agree with its leaders.

They want to see change.

So they help the enemy.

How?

By giving away their nation's secrets.

Some spy for money.

They are not *loyal* to anyone.

Secrets are worth big money.

For some, that is all that matters.

13

Spying goes on all the time.
But it increases during wars.
Countries fight.
Each wants to win.
They want to know about the enemy.
Spies help them do that.
They learn about battle plans.
Find where the enemy is weak.

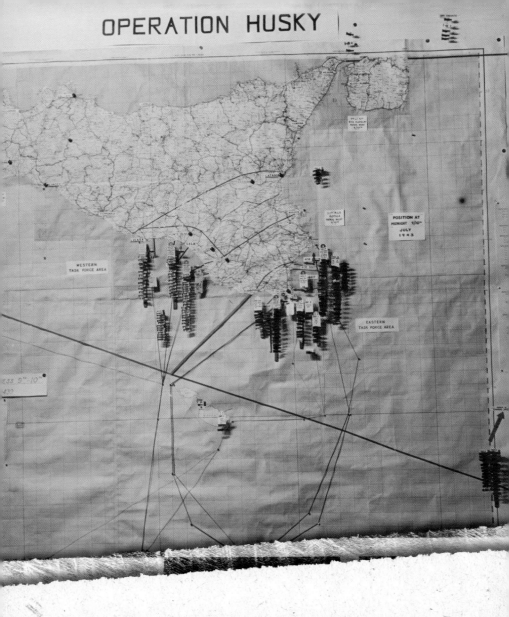

Spies have helped win wars.
Some we know about.
Many we never will.
Staying hidden keeps them alive.

Businesses use spies too.

They spy on their *rivals*.

Companies have many secrets.

New things they are making.

Inventions.

Spies try to steal them.

Or copy them.

Spying is big business.

Chapter 3
SPIES AMONG US

Most nations use spies.
Leaders need them.
They need facts.
Some facts are hard to get.
Spies can get them.

The United States has many spies.

Some work for the CIA.

The Central Intelligence Agency.

Its job is to know things.

Things no one else knows.

The CIA trains spies.

It teaches them languages.

How to hack computers.

Listen in on people talking.

CIA spies go to other countries.

They learn secrets.

The president uses those secrets.

Knowing them can help protect
the country.

19

U.S. spies also work for the NSA.
The National Security Agency.
Its spies *eavesdrop* on people.
They read e-mails.

SPY LINGO: HANDLER

Everyone has a boss, even
spies. A handler tells a spy
what to do.

Listen in on phone calls.
What are they looking for?
Criminals.
Terrorists.
Spies from other countries.
Anyone who might hurt the U.S.

Who can be a spy?

Anyone.

A neighbor.

Teacher.

Uncle or aunt.

You wouldn't know.

That's the point.

Spies work *undercover*.
They hide who they are.
No one *suspects* them.
That's how they can
learn secrets.

23

Spies can kill too.

They may kill enemies.

Or people who find out about them.

Some spies use poison.

Or secret weapons.

They are trained to do this.

They learn *self-defense*.

How to wear *disguises*.

They have to be ready.

Anything can happen.

TOOLS OF THE TRADE

British spies used a flashlight gun. It did not light up the dark. It shot bullets.

Spies have to be careful.

They work in other countries.

What if they get caught?

They can be arrested.

Put on trial.

Even put to death.

Yet people still spy.

They take the risks.

Some even become famous.

Chapter 4
MATA HARI: QUEEN OF SPIES

World War I.

It ripped Europe apart.

Germany was France's enemy.

Margaretha Zell wanted to help.

She wanted to be a German spy.

So she went to spy school.

Then she moved to Paris.

She became Mata Hari.

A woman who loved to dance.

IDENTIFICATION ORDER
NO. 82563

NAME: Margaretha Zell
(Mata Hari)

SPY FOR: Germany

TIME PERIOD: World War I
(1914-1918)

French soldiers liked her.

They told her secrets.

She told them lies.

Some didn't believe her.

They put Mata Hari in jail.

Die or help them.

It was her choice.

Mata Hari said okay.

She would spy on the Germans.

Another lie.

She was still loyal to Germany.

She was jailed again.

And sentenced to die.

The day arrived.

Mata Hari was not afraid.

She wore a new dress.

New gloves.

"I am ready," she said.

The soldiers took aim.

She blew them a kiss.

Shots rang out.

Mata Hari died.

Iran.

A country in the Middle East.

1979.

The U.S. was a friend of Iran's leader.

His people did not like him.

They pushed him out of power.

He came to the U.S.

That made many people mad.

IDENTIFICATION ORDER
NO. 76492

NAME: Tony Mendez

SPY FOR: United States

TIME PERIOD: 1979

TOP SECRET
CONFIDENTIAL

A mob circled the U.S. *embassy*.

It was in Tehran.

Iran's capital.

They stormed the building.

They took *hostages*.

Six escaped.

Canadians hid them.

But they could not do it for long.

The Americans had to find a way out.

Tony Mendez had an idea.
He was a spy for the CIA.
It was a crazy plan.
Make a movie in Iran.
The movie was a fake.
Argo. A sci-fi film.
He said he was Canadian.
That was a lie too.
One the Iranians believed.

Mendez gave the Americans fake IDs.

He taught them to act like moviemakers.

Then it was time to go.

They went to the airport.

A guard looked at them.

He went into a room.

Would they be caught?

The guard came back.

He had a cup of tea.

He was thirsty, not *suspicious*.

The plane took off.

Mendez got a medal.

No one knew about the rescue.

Not for years.

TOOLS OF THE TRADE

Pencils are used to write.
But spies can turn them into
weapons. British spies used them
to hide cross-shaped blades.

Chapter 6

WILD ROSE: SOUTHERN SPY

Rose O'Neal Greenhow.

"Wild Rose."

She lived in Washington, D.C.

It was during the Civil War.

The South fought the North.

The South wanted to be its own country.

Wild Rose wanted that too.

She couldn't be a soldier.

So she became a Southern spy.

IDENTIFICATION ORDER
NO. 96693

NAME: Rose O'Neal Greenhow

SPY FOR: The South

TIME PERIOD: U.S. Civil War (1861-1865)

Wild Rose loved parties.

She danced.

Sang.

Talked to all the right people.

They shared secrets.

She wrote them down.

Wild Rose learned things.
Like the enemy's battle plans.
She sent a secret message south.
A general read it.
His soldiers were ready.
The enemy came.
The South won the battle.

The North found out.
The army told Rose to stay home.
She kept spying.
They sent her to prison.
Friends visited her.
She gave them notes.
They carried them out in their hair.

The North won the war.
But Rose was a hero in the South.
She later wrote a book.
It was about being a spy.

in
the
as a
sation
g was

ket to
e, and

would

Chapter 7
MOE BERG:
THE CATCHER
IS A SPY

Strike three! You're out!
Moe Berg heard that a lot.
He was a baseball player.
But not a very good one.
He played with Babe Ruth.
The best in the game.
Both joined an all-star team.

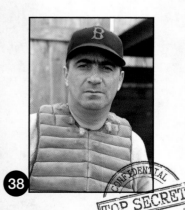

IDENTIFICATION ORDER
NO. 29492

NAME: Moe Berg

SPY FOR: United States

TIME PERIOD: Word War II
(1939-1945)

CONFIDENTIAL
TOP SECRET
CONFIDENTIAL

Babe Ruth made sense.
But why Moe Berg?
Moe was a catcher.
But he was also a U.S. spy.
No one knew.

The team went to Japan.
That was in 1934.
Moe slipped away from games.
He took pictures of Tokyo.

War came in 1941.
The U.S. fought Japan.
The military used Moe's photos.
Planes bombed Tokyo.

Moe did more.

1944 came.

The war was nearly over.

Germany was another enemy.

It was working on a new weapon.

An *atomic* bomb.

The U.S. was worried.

Moe was sent on a mission.

He went to Italy.

A German scientist was there.

He was giving a speech.

Moe had dinner with him.

He asked questions.

Learned they were not close

to making the bomb.

What if they had been?

Mo had orders.

He had a gun.

He would have killed the scientist.

SPY LINGO: BUG

Bugs are tiny hidden microphones. Spies use them to listen to their enemies.

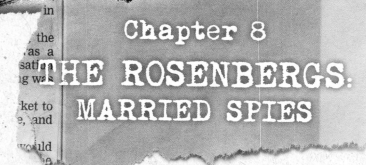

Chapter 8
THE ROSENBERGS:
MARRIED SPIES

World War II ended in 1945.

The U.S. had the atomic bomb.

No other country did.

Joseph Stalin wanted the bomb.

He led the *Soviet Union*.

He called on two spies.

Julius and Ethel Rosenberg.

They were Americans.

But they were part of a Soviet spy ring.

IDENTIFICATION ORDER
NO. 63862

NAME: Julius and Ethel
      Rosenberg

SPY FOR: Soviet Union

TIME PERIOD: 1950s

CONFIDENTIAL
TOP SECRET
CONFIDENTIAL

Julius and Ethel were regular people.

Julius worked for the U.S. Army.

Ethel's brother was a scientist.

He helped build the atomic bomb.

He gave them secrets.

Secrets they passed to the Soviets.

U.S. agents broke up the spy ring.
The Rosenbergs were arrested.
They said they weren't spies.

There was a trial.
They were found guilty.
Julius and Ethel went to prison.
They were put to death in 1953.

Chapter 9
ALDRICH AMES: DOUBLE AGENT

Aldrich Ames.

He was a spy.

He worked for the CIA.

Ames found Russian spies.

He got them to be *double agents*.

They spied on the Soviets.

They worked for the U.S.

IDENTIFICATION ORDER
NO. 99273

NAME: Aldrich Ames

SPY FOR: United States and Soviet Union

TIME PERIOD: 1980s

45

Ames needed money.
He visited the Soviets.
He sold them names.
U.S. spies in Russia.
The Russians jailed some.
They killed others.
Ames made millions.

Ames spied for years.
But he was caught.
Today, Ames is in prison.
Guilty of treason.

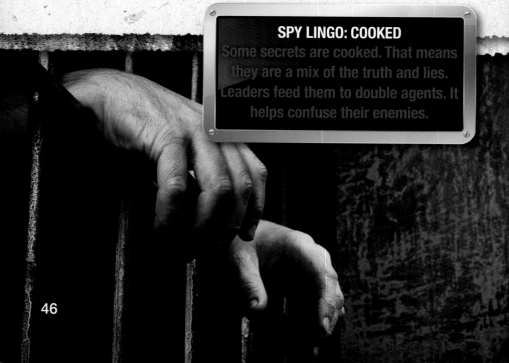

SPY LINGO: COOKED
Some secrets are cooked. That means they are a mix of the truth and lies. Leaders feed them to double agents. It helps confuse their enemies.

All these spies.

Men.

Women.

They risked their lives.

Some for their nation.

Some for money.

People still spy today.

But they have machines to help.

Spy satellites circle Earth.

They take photos.

Spies also use *drones*.

Flying robots.

They snap photos.

Get secrets on film.

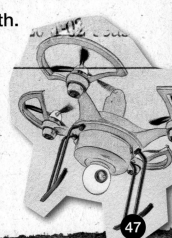

Today's spies help fight terror groups.
Drug dealers.
Criminals.
They are moles.
They join these groups.
Pass on their secrets.

Some spies use computers.
They go online.
Attack other computers.
Shut them down.
Steal secrets.
Read e-mails.
Take videos.

Do you know a spy?
You might.
But you would never know.
A good spy stays secret.

atomic: using the energy that is made when atoms split apart

criminal: a person who has broken the law

disguise: clothes or makeup worn to look like someone else

double agent: spy who pretends to work for one government but really works for another

drone: remote-controlled aircraft

eavesdrop: to listen without someone knowing

embassy: an office of one country in another country

espionage: things done to find out secrets from enemies

hostage: a person captured by people who want something in return

information: facts or details about something

loyal: having or showing support for someone

rival: a company in the same business as another company

self-defense: skills that let people protect themselves when attacked

Soviet Union: a nation in Eastern Europe and north Asia that was made up of many states

spying: trying to secretly get information about a country or group

suspects: thinks that someone is lying or guilty of a crime

suspicious: on guard; not sure someone is telling the truth

terrorist: a person who uses violence to scare people into doing something

traitor: one who betrays their own country

undercover: pretending to be a member of a group to learn their secrets

AREA 51

Chapter 5
SPY PLANES

It was the 1950s.
The U.S. was at a *standoff*.
It had nuclear weapons.
So did the Soviet Union.
Each country spied on the other.

DID YOU KNOW?
The Soviet Union shot down a U-2 in 1960. They used a missile.

The CIA wanted a spy plane to help.
The U-2 was made.
It was tested at Area 51.
It could fly very high.
So high it would not be seen.

26

27

Chapter 6
MORE SECRET PROJECTS

Spy planes.
We know about some of them.
Those used in the past.
But not today.
The military is always making new models.
They want them faster.
More quiet.
Harder to find.
And they must keep them secret.

Is Area 51 still hiding spy tools today?
Many think it is.
We can't know.
But there are *rumors*.
Ideas of new secret projects.

Photos show Area 51 buildings.
But many think there is more there.
Underground.
Secret floors.

Movies have shown this idea.
So have TV shows.
Secret labs.
Captured aliens.
Captured alien ships.
Is any of it true?
No one knows.

UNDERGROUND HALLWAYS

DID YOU KNOW?
A movie came out in 1996.
Independence Day. It showed secret
levels of Area 51. A captured alien
and a spaceship were there.

red rhino books®

NONFICTION

9781680210293

9781680210286

9781680210309

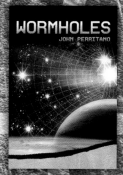

9781680210330

9781680210361

9781680210323

9781680210316

9781680210538

9781680210347

9781680210354

9781680210491

9781680210521

9781680210378

9781680210484

MORE
TITLES
COMING
SOON